THE TOWN

Where was the town? When did people live there? How big was it? What did it look like? These are some of the questions archaeologists investigating Hamwic want to answer.

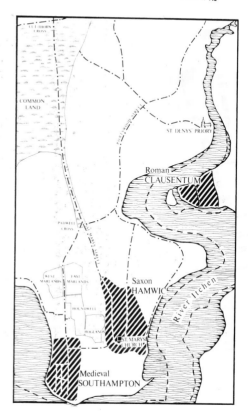

Archaeologists have been able to define the limits of the town by systematic excavations in the St Mary's area of Southampton. To the east of Hamwic lay the River Itchen. To the south and north-east, occupation was restricted by marshes. On the west side, however, the boundary was marked by a ditch three metres wide and one and half metres deep (about ten feet by five feet). Nearby houses did not spread beyond this even after the ditch had been filled in. More than 100 acres of flat open ground on the west bank of the River Itchen were built over to form the town of Hamwic. This was quite a substantial town comparing favourably in size with other Saxon towns such as London, Canterbury, Ipswich, and York.

The site had not previously been intensely occupied. The earlier Roman town of Clausentum lay to the north-east on the eastern shore of the River Itchen, at Bitterne Manor. Later, the Medieval town was established on the gravel peninsula at the mouth of the River Test.

Establishing dates for Hamwic is not easy. The earliest document refers to the town in AD 721, the last in AD 840. These tell us very little about what went on in the town, but at least they show that Hamwic was in existence throughout most of the 8th century and for part of the 9th century. Coins found in the town provide useful dating evidence. Some of the earliest coins

found at Hamwic, known as sceattas, are datable to around AD 700-10, while the later pennies carry the names of kings or bishops and can be dated through documentary reference. Almost the last of these pennies was minted around AD 850. Pottery, a much more common find on excavations, is invaluable as rough dating evidence. The archaeologist relies on recognisable changes in technique and style over time to give a relative sequence of pottery types. The appearance of distinctive types of pottery suggests an early 8th century date for the beginning of Hamwic and a late 9th century date for its disappearance.

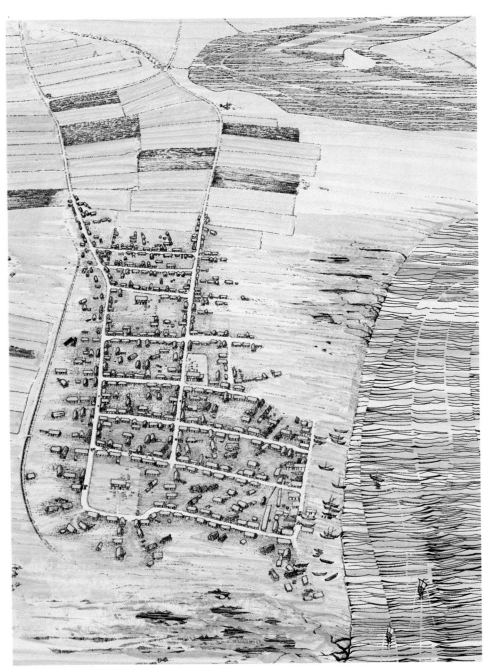

An artist's impression of Hamwic about AD 750.

An artist's impression of the Six Dials site about AD 750.

Archaeological excavation provides clear evidence of the physical nature and appearance of the town. Large-scale open excavations at the Six Dials site revealed a clear plan of this part of the town. A major gravelled street up to fifteen metres (fifty feet) wide ran north-south beneath the present line of St Mary's Road. East-west streets running off this major thoroughfare were five metres (seventeen feet) wide and equally well gravelled. All the streets were well maintained and regularly resurfaced. Houses fronted onto the streets. Between the houses, alleyways led to yards and more buildings standing further back from the streets. In those back yards people dug large numbers of rubbish pits – over 400 have been excavated at the Six Dials site alone.

Excavations throughout the town show that a similar dense occupation appeared all over Hamwic, grouped around gravel streets. The line of several of these still survive as modern roads: St Mary Street, St Mary's Road, Derby Road, Marine Parade, and Chapel Road. Together with other streets that did not continue in use after Hamwic had gone, these formed part of a regular grid pattern of streets.

There is a stark contrast between well maintained streets and the clutter of individual properties. Behind the houses, the alleyways and yard surfaces were shortlived, surviving only as long as the property they served, and in time being dug through by pits. The streets, however, were maintained throughout the life of the town. The regularity of street plan suggests some control in the town's foundation and development. Was the town planned and laid out at one time, controlled by a central authority? An even distribution of early pottery and coins over the whole of Hamwic would suggest that it was laid out at one time, or, if it grew from a core, it did so very rapidly.

How could a large town grow so quickly? There are various possible explanations, the most likely being that the political and economic stability which existed under Ine, king of Wessex (688-726), favoured the establishment and growth of Hamwic. Some central authority would have been necessary to maintain control over street planning and maintenance. Royal officers may have controlled the development of the town; but it is equally possible that the authority resided in regular meetings of the townsfolk similar to the medieval Court Leet. Such is the nature of archaeological evidence that these questions will probably never be resolved.

The physical characteristics of Hamwic – its size, density of occupation, and organised plan – show clearly that it was a town rather than a hamlet or village. But was it a town in an economic sense, based on trade and industry rather than agriculture? To answer this question we need to know what the people of Hamwic did. Were they primarily farmers, or were they involved in industries and trade, with the countryside around Hamwic providing the food and necessary raw materials for the urban inhabitants?

INTERNATIONAL TRADE

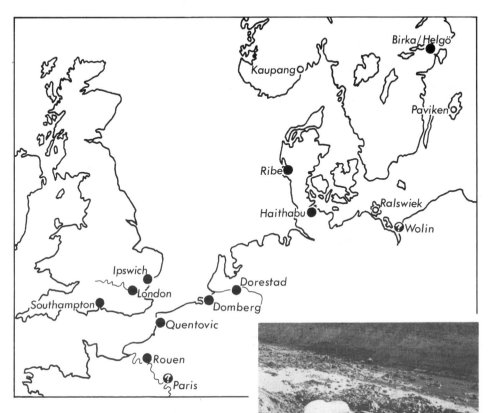

The later 7th century saw the development of a number of trading centres along Europe's north-west coast. London, York, and Ipswich were trading with similar towns across the Channel and North Sea. Eventually, these towns extended from Rouen in Normandy and Quentovic in northern France, up through Dorestad in Holland, through Haithabu and Domburg in Denmark, to Birka in Sweden. The archaeological evidence shows that the people of Hamwic took part in this trade.

The remains of a 10th century ship found at Graveney in Kent.

The Evidence

Coins

Nearly 200 Saxon coins have been recovered from excavations in Hamwic, a far greater number than from any other Saxon site. The very large number of coins alone provides a strong argument for Hamwic being a trading centre with a monetary economy.

A sceatta minted in Hamwic.

A 'Wodan Monster' sceatta.

The majority of coins are sceattas whose primary use throughout Europe in the 8th century was for trade. Sceattas are small coins made of silver. Roughly half of the sceattas found in Hamwic were minted in the town. These coins appear to have been used as a form of currency only within the town as they are very rarely found elsewhere. The number of sceattas minted in Hamwic must have been considerable. Estimates of upwards of two million have been made. If these are correct, the amount of trade must have been very great. The largest number of coins were minted during the middle of the 8th century from about AD 720-80. This was probably the period of Hamwic's greatest trading activity.

The sceattas that were not minted in Hamwic indicate who the town's trading partners were. The 'Porcupine' and 'Wodan Monster' sceattas, so called because of the designs on the coins, show that links existed with the places that minted them; with Dorestad, the area of the Rhine mouth, and perhaps Denmark. Other sceattas found in Hamwic were minted elsewhere in England; mainly in Kent, London, and the Midlands.

A 'Porcupine' sceatta.

Pottery

Pottery is a very common find on excavation sites. It can be invaluable not only for dating but also as evidence for trade. The regional source of a pot can often be identified, especially if the pottery is distinctive in form, decoration, or fabric. The majority of domestic pottery found in Hamwic, such as cooking pots and storage jars, were made locally. The finer wheelmade wares, however, were imported from the Continent. These pots, often in the form of spouted pitchers and bowls, came mainly from pottery centres in northern France around Rouen, Amiens, and Quentovic. (Some of the Continental imports are not found in other English towns.) The pots may have been brought in as containers of traded commodities such as wine or oil; or they may have been imported by foreign traders residing in Hamwic, who preferred their own fine tablewares to the coarser locally produced pottery.

Other Imports

Other objects have been found in Hamwic which indicate trade with the Continent. Particular types of stone can be characterised and their sources identified. Lava quernstones, used for grinding grain, were widely traded at this time. The stone was quarried in the Eifel mountains near Mayen, and shipped with other goods to trading towns where they were finished. Complete lava quernstones are rare but fragments found in Hamwic amount to over 72kg (158 lb) in weight. A small number of Hamwic's whetstones, used for sharpening knives, are made of mica-schist and were imported from Scandinavia. Glass was also imported from the production centres in the Rhine valley but no complete vessels have survived, though plenty of fragments do. It is possible that these coloured or decorated glass fragments, known as cullet, were imported for remelting and making into beads.

LOCAL INDUSTRIES

But Hamwic did not exist only for long-distance trade between the various kingdoms of Saxon England, Merovingian France, and the rest of north-west Europe. The town was also a centre of production, with craft industries serving the local population.

The Evidence

Metalworking

Large concentrations of smithing slag, hammerscale, and hearths are evidence enough to show that iron objects were being made in Hamwic. Slag, the waste product from melting iron, and hammerscale, small flecks of iron which fly off when it is being hammered, have been found in large quantities throughout the town. However, there is little evidence that iron was being smelted in the town. It was probably brought into the town in the form of cakes or rods ready for working into objects. At the Six Dials site two areas were found which had hearths and large spreads of slag and hammerscale. These areas, both located at street junctions, probably represent smiths' workshops. In both areas the hearths and debris had lain within wooden structures, recognisable in plan. These seem to have been open-fronted workshops. The blacksmith's tools, including anvils, hammers, and tongs, have not been found in Hamwic; but these would have been very valuable items and are not likely to have been lost or left behind.

Top: Two keys.
Centre: Fragment of a wool comb.
Bottom: Three knife blades.

An artist's impression of a smith's workshop based on the plan exposed at the Six Dials site, shown below.

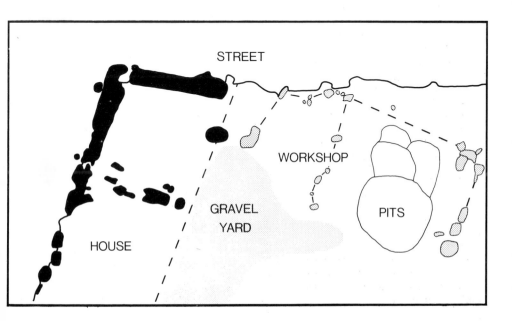

What were the blacksmiths making? Assuming that the majority of iron objects found in Hamwic were being made there, a wide variety of different items were being produced by the blacksmiths of the town. Many of the objects were tools such as knives, shears, chisels, axes, and woolcombs. A large number of knives found in Hamwic have fine steel cutting edges welded onto the main body of the blade showing the high quality of work involved in their manufacture. In addition there were smaller everyday items such as nails, rivets, locks, and keys. It seems clear that the blacksmiths of Hamwic were highly skilled specialists producing iron objects for the people of the town and perhaps also for the surrounding countryside.

A group of bronze objects.

Crucibles for melting bronze in.

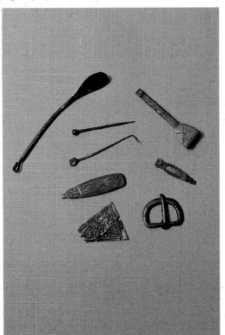

There is also evidence for the working of other metals on a smaller scale. Crucibles and moulds show that bronze objects were being made in Hamwic. They were often small, decorative items such as dress pins, strap ends, buckles, tweezers, and decorative mounts. Some of these objects display intricate designs requiring skilful techniques. A stone with traces of gold and mercury on it show that at least one metalworker in Hamwic was gilding some of the more decorative objects. Crucibles have also been found containing traces of silver and gold, though items other than coins made from precious metals are rare.

Glass Working

The presence in Hamwic of large quantities of glass fragments and several glass rod wasters·(glass which has been remelted and pulled into a rod ready for reworking) suggests that glass was being collected, remelted, and worked into other objects such as beads. Glass was rare in Saxon England, and broken glass, known as cullet, was in itself a valuable commodity.

It is even possible that glass vessels were being made in Hamwic. (This would be a great rarity if it is true, since very few glass-production centres have been identified in Saxon England.) Although no furnace has been found, the distinct form and colour of glass beakers with a type of decoration unique to Hamwic hint at the possibility that these vessels were being made by craftspeople resident in the town.

A selection of decorated glass fragments.

Bone and Antler Working

Animal bone and deer antler were frequently used in Saxon England for the manufacture of many objects. Combs, sometimes highly decorated, were perhaps the most common objects made of bone and antler. Tools for cloth making were often made of bone – needles, spindles, spindlewhorls, and threadpickers. The large numbers of sawn offcuts of animal bone and deer antler testify to these objects being made by artisans throughout the town.

A decorated bone plaque.

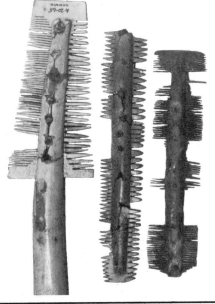

Cattle bones were most frequently used, whereas objects made of sheep or pig bones are unusual. Antler was used to make many of the combs and also dies or stamps which were used to decorate pottery. Found at the Six Dials site was a complete but unfinished bone comb. All the pieces had been cut to size and prepared but had not been assembled. From these pieces we can see exactly how the combs were constructed. Various types of combs were made, including single- and double-sided combs with handles and double-sided combs without handles. The double-sided combs were made by placing flat segments of bone or antler between two connecting plates. Several holes were drilled and iron rivets were then inserted to hold the flat segments and connecting plates together. Any decoration of the connecting plates or handles was usually done before rivetting. Finally, the teeth were cut into the flat segments.

An unfinished comb.

Wool and Cloth Industry

Most of the evidence for the production of wool and for clothmaking comes indirectly from the bones of sheep and objects used in clothmaking. Only a few fragments of woollen cloth have survived whereas objects associated with cloth making are common finds.

Information recovered from the bones of sheep about their size and age at death clearly indicate that the animals were being kept for their wool, and not slaughtered at an early age for their meat. This evidence shows too that wool production grew in importance throughout the life of Hamwic: more sheep were being kept, and were being specially bred to be larger.

Spinning and weaving were commonly done by women. After it was washed, the wool was combed using a woolcomb. The wool was then spun using a simple spindle and a weight called a spindle whorl. Whorls made of animal bone and antler, and a few

Spindle and whorl made from antler and bone.

made of clay and stone, have been found in Hamwic. The wool would have been attached to the spindle and as this was spun and dropped the wool was pulled out and twisted into a yarn.

The yarn was then woven into cloth on an upright loom. Items associated with weaving have been found throughout Hamwic. These include clay loomweights, used to keep the warp (the vertical threads) straight and taut, and bone threadpickers for beating the weft (the horizontal threads) into place. Very fine cloth could be woven, as the few fragments of cloth found have shown. Up to twenty threads per square centimetre are the sign of extremely finely woven cloth such as woollen worsted. Sewing implements are plentiful: large and small bone needles have been found throughout the town, as well as a few iron needles.

Tablet weaving was also carried out in

Hamwic, as the recovery of one tablet shows. The tablet was a square plate made of antler with a hole in each corner. Using a pack of such tablets, several strands of yarn would be woven together into a colourful and decorative edging which could be woven or sewn onto the main cloth.

Wool and cloth were important exports from the later town of Medieval Southampton, the products on which much of the town's wealth was based. It is possible that this trade in wool and cloth had its origins in Saxon times. However, very little is known about what the people of Hamwic were exporting and few documentary references exist which list Saxon exports as they do for Medieval Southampton.

Baked clay loomweights.

Other Industries

There is little or no evidence for the other trades, industries, and activities that the people of Hamwic were undoubtedly involved in. A great many things would have been made in materials such as wood and leather which only very rarely survive for many hundreds of years in the ground. Leather, like cloth, would have been a very important material for clothing: in waterlogged conditions, such as at Viking York, leather shoes are commonly found. In such conditions, where wood also is preserved, wooden bowls, buckets, and barrels are seen to be commonplace.

The different craft activities appear to have been carried out at home: there is no evidence of industrial zoning in the town, nor any signs of social stratification. The wealthy and less wealthy, the boneworker, the blacksmith, and the weaver lived side by side in a seemingly egalitarian society. This picture built from the archaeological evidence is at odds with the documentary evidence which suggests that Saxon society was quite rigidly structured. For the moment, this contradiction cannot be resolved.

A wooden bucket which survived in waterlogged conditions in Hamwic.

Summary

The evidence shows quite clearly that Hamwic was a town in both its physical characteristics and in its economic role. The settled population of Hamwic was not involved in primary farming activities. The general impression of the town is of a well organised artisan community engaged in long-distance trade and small-scale industrial production.

DAILY LIFE AND LIVING CONDITIONS

What would it have been like to live in Hamwic? What were the houses like? What food did people eat? What clothes did they wear? And how long did they live? These questions can be answered by looking again at the material remains left in the ground and asking different questions about it.

The Evidence

In The Home

The houses were fairly densely packed together and were aligned along the street or set further back in the yards behind. They have left their mark in the ground in the form of post-holes and gulleys. The plans of the houses show them to have been rectangular in shape, between ten to twelve metres (thirty-three to thirty-nine feet) long and up to five metres (seventeen feet) wide. The post-holes and gulleys held wooden uprights forming the frames of single-storeyed houses. Walls were made from

The postholes belong to buildings fronting onto a gravel street (at top). The larger holes are rubbish pits.

An artist's impression of a Saxon house based on house plans exposed at the Six Dials site, shown below.

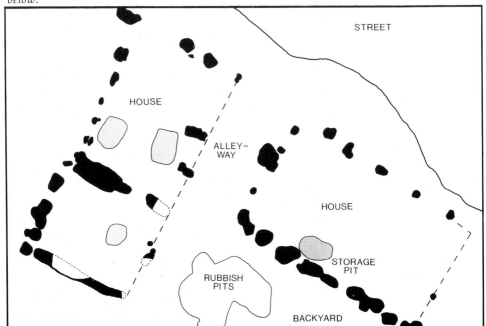

STREET

HOUSE

ALLEY-
WAY

HOUSE

STORAGE
PIT

RUBBISH
PITS

BACKYARD

*A pottery lamp encrusted
with the residues of fish oil*

wattle fencing, set around the uprights and thickly daubed with clay. To weatherproof the houses, the daub walls were limewashed. None of the houses in Hamwic was built of stone. No roofing slate or tile has been found, which suggests that the roof was probably made of thatch, or possibly wooden shingles. The houses were quite substantial and each may have stood for three decades or more. Pressure of space and density of occupation in the town led to the rebuilding of houses. Some houses were rebuilt as many as five times on the same site.

Inside, the house would probably have been dark, smoky, and possibly quite damp. Whether or not the houses had windows is not known; but if there were windows they certainly would not have had glass in them. The houses could have been lit by burning fish oil in simple lamps made of stone or clay. Adding to the atmosphere in the house would have been the fire, set on a simple clay hearth. The smoke would have drifted slowly up and out of the house through the eaves and roof, filling the home with the smells of cooking and smouldering wood.

The floors were made simply of compacted clay, and possibly covered with rushes to keep them dry. The absence of any household rubbish on the floor shows that they were kept clean. Small storage pits, lined with wattle or wooden planks, have been found in some houses. They may have been used in a similar way to larders today. As for furniture, none survives in Hamwic but it is unlikely that people would have sat and slept directly on the clay floors.

Some houses had one large room whereas others were divided into two by means of a simple partition. As well as a home, the houses were often workshops where the people carried out their trades and crafts.

Behind the houses were yards which would no doubt have been used for growing vegetables, and for keeping chickens; perhaps also pigs. Rubbish pits dug in the yards may indicate boundary lines between properties. Over 400 rubbish pits have been excavated at Six Dials alone. The pits were often very deep, occasionally up to three metres (ten feet) deep. Such a depth suggests pressure of space in the town and contributes to the picture of dense occupation. The pits were initially used for the disposal of sewage which was sealed by a layer of clay to stop the smell. They would then have been slowly filled with the rubbish from nearby homes, perhaps over a period of several decades as the original contents slowly subsided. Rural excavations have shown that the Saxons cleared their pits out periodically spreading the decomposing compost, along with other household items, onto the fields. However, there is very little evidence to suggest the people of Hamwic were doing the same. This is surprising as the compost would have been a very valuable resource.

Fresh water, of vital importance to any community, was obtained from wells dug in the back yards. The wells were dug away from the rubbish pits so as not to contaminate the water. Upwards of 35 wells have been excavated in Hamwic. A well was dug by digging a large pit and then continuing downwards with a smaller shaft until water was reached. Some wells were over four metres (thirteen feet) deep. The shaft was lined to stop it collapsing, with wattle, planks and old wooden casks. The surrounding pit was then backfilled, leaving only the shaft open. A wooden bucket on the end of a rope was probably the means by which the water was drawn. Excavations have often revealed the bottom of the wells to be very clean, suggesting they were covered to stop rubbish falling in and also to save the unsuspecting passerby from a similar fate.

Timbers surviving at the bottom of a well at the Six Dials site.

Clothing and Personal Dress

It is not easy to imagine how a Saxon living in Hamwic might have dressed. The few pieces of cloth and textile that do survive show that clothes were made of quite finely woven wool coloured red, blue, or yellow with natural dyes such as madder, woad, and weld. The garments may have been decorated also with simple braids and decorative edging woven on tablets.

The main evidence for daily dress is to be found in manuscript illustrations which indicate that tunics were commonly worn with leather shoes to cover the feet. Firmer evidence survives for the decoration and fastenings on clothing. Bronze pins used to fasten garments are common finds in Hamwic. Copper buckles and brooches too would have been used as fastenings, while strap ends – ornate mounts on the ends of laces and belts – were frequently decorated with animal and floral designs.

Decorated bronze pins and strapends.

A Saxon Meal

What sort of food did the people of Hamwic eat? The evidence lies in the animal bones, shell, charred grains, and preserved seeds which the archaeologist must carefully recover. Vegetables, cereals and some tough beef, eaten as a pottage or stew with bread, would probably have been the staple diet for most people in Hamwic. This would have included foodstuffs preserved by salting them.

Unlike Medieval townsfolk, the people of Hamwic ate a fairly limited variety of foods. The basic meat content of the diet consisted mainly of beef, with some pork and mutton. Only a small percentage of the animal bones are of poultry such as chicken or duck, and the large varieties of wild species eaten in the Medieval town – for

example partridge, goose, dove, hare, and pigeon – are entirely absent.

An examination of the animal bones shows that the meat itself was not of prime quality. The age and size of the cattle bones, for instance, show that they had already worked a hard life as draught animals in the fields. By the time the animals were driven into the town to be slaughtered for food, their tough meat was fit only for the stewing pot.

If the meat did not afford much variety, there was certainly a greater choice of plant foods both cultivated and wild. Plant remains are preserved by the processes of watterlogging, charring, and mineralization.

Locally produced cooking pots from Hamwic.

The majority of seeds found in Hamwic have been preserved by mineralisation – where the organic structure of the seed is replaced by minerals from the ground. Charred grains are not common but many seeds, preserved by constant damp, are recovered from the waterlogged soils at the bottom of deep pits.

Bread was a very important part of the diet, and cereal grains have been found throughout the town. Wheat, barley, oats, and rye would all have been used to make bread. The cereal grains found in the town were fully processed, which suggests that they were brought into the town ready for grinding into flour. It is likely that each household ground its own flour on a quern and made its own bread on the hearth or in an oven at home.

Some food may have been deliberately grown on plots in the town: these include carrots, broad beans, field beans, and peas, as well as flavourings such as thyme, parsley, mint, and mustard. Many of the vegetables, such as nettles, fat-hen, and sorrel, were wild and could have been collected from any wasteland in the area.

A great variety of soft fruits, such as pear, raspberry, blackberry, apple, plum, and cherry, were available in the town.

Fish and shellfish, although not eaten in large quantities, would have supplemented and added some variety to the diet. Abundant deposits of oyster shells as well as some mussel, winkle, and cockle shells, show that shellfish were being eaten. All the species of fish identified from Hamwic – eel, trout, salmon, herring, mackerel, cod, bream, and plaice – could have been caught in the estuarine waters around Hamwic.

With a ready supply of meat and a wide variety of plant food the people of Hamwic would have had a well balanced and healthy diet. The distribution of animals and plant remains across the town suggests no pattern of obvious wealth or poverty as the same types of food seem to have been available to everyone.

Children from Southampton experiment with cooking a meal the Saxon way.

Health and Sickness

The human skeleton provides a useful insight into the life of someone living in Hamwic. From studying the bones it is possible to estimate how long people lived, what diseases they suffered from, what was their general state of health, and what type of food they ate.

Human teeth are good indicators of the type of food being eaten. A quite severe rate of attrition – the wearing down of the tooth cusps – evident in the people of Hamwic suggests that much of the food they were eating was coarse and gritty. Dental diseases such as caries and tooth loss were also quite common. These diseases reflect the dietary habits of a people over a number of years and suggest that carbohydrates – cereals and bread – featured quite highly in the diet.

On the whole, however, the people of Hamwic seem to have been fairly healthy. Their average heights, 1.7 metres (5 feet 7 inches) for men and 1.64 metres (5 feet 4 inches) for women, show them to have been healthy and well fed. Their life span too, though surprisingly short to us today, is very similar to that of other Saxon groups in

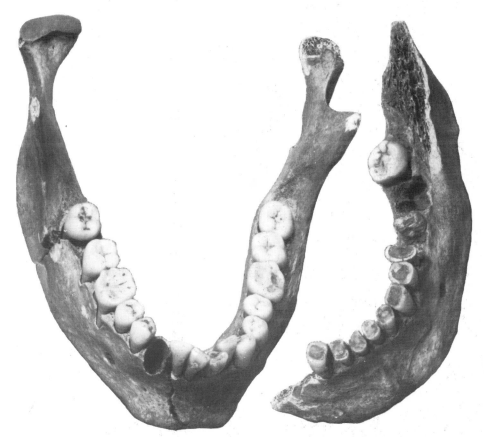

Patterns of wear on the teeth of a young person (left) and an old person (right).

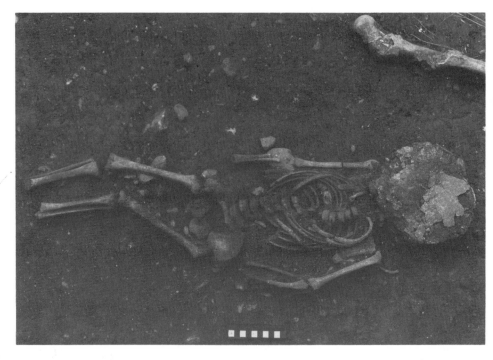

A child burial at Hamwic aged approximately 5 years.

England. Men lived 40 years on average and women had a shorter life expectancy, living on average only 35 years. These average life spans, and the fact that they were perfectly normal, highlight the hard physical life led by the inhabitants.

Women had shorter lives than men largely due to the dangers of pregnancy. Frequent pregnancies not only meant great physical stress but also demanded a more nutritious diet for the woman throughout her pregnancy and during breast feeding. If these demands were not being met they would seriously affect the life expectancy of the woman. Children too were vulnerable. Infant deaths were common and up to thirty per cent of the population died before the age of ten. These childhood deaths were often the result of chronic diaorrhoea leading to malnutrition.

Physical stress, the result of hard work in both men and women, is reflected in the high incidence of arthritic diseases: arthritis, particularly noticeable in the spinal vertebrae, was universal in people over thirty years of age.

DEATH AND BURIAL

The people of Hamwic were Christians. As today, the most powerful and visible symbol of Christianity was the church. In Hamwic at least one church and several small cemeteries have been excavated.

The church, recognised by its ground plan, consisted of a simple rectangular nave and chancel and would have been built of timber. Fragments of window glass, found when excavating the site, suggest that the church had had glazed windows.

Excavations in the graveyard around this church, and other small graveyards in Hamwic, have shown how the dead were buried and some of the attitudes towards the dead. The bodies were laid in wooden coffins and placed in shallow graves aligned east-west in the Christian fashion. Unlike earlier pagan burials no grave goods accompanied the person into the grave. The dead were neatly disposed of, laid in rows with the graves marked by mounds of earth and some with more elaborate gravemarkers.

All the graveyards excavated have been small, the largest having had perhaps 100 burials. Excavations have uncovered only

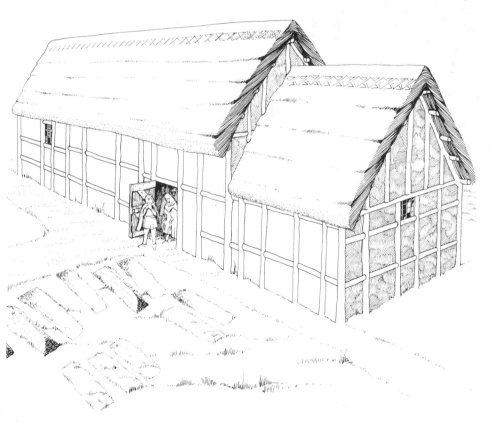

An artist's impression of a church and cemetery excavated in Hamwic.

about 200 burials, a very small proportion of
what must have been a fairly large
population. The majority of the people were
probably buried around a church where the
church of St Mary stands today. In the 8th
century a simple wooden church would
have stood where the great stone church
now stands. Mentioned in a South
Stoneham charter of 1045 as 'that minster of
(Ham)wic', in 1225 the church of St Mary
was recognised by the pope as the mother
church of Southampton.

THE LOST TOWN

What happened to Hamwic? This is perhaps the most pressing question for archaeologists today, a question still not fully answered.

Hamwic's decline is reflected in the lesser density of occupation from about the middle of the 9th century onwards. The number of buildings fall off quite considerably and the amount of occupation debris declines. The streets too begin to be encroached on, with occasional pits being dug through them. A small community did continue to live in Hamwic but the place no longer had the characteristics of a town. The church where St Mary's now stands, some of the streets, and a few buildings would have

been all that remained of Hamwic in the 10th century.

Much of the demise of Hamwic can be related to a general pattern of disruption and insecurity throughout northern Europe in the middle of the 9th century. Civil wars following the division of Charlemagne's empire in the first half of the 9th century probably had an effect on trade. The slightly later Viking raids of the 830s and 840s may have affected Hamwic more so. The Anglo-Saxon Chronicle records that in 840 an attack was made on Hamwic. Perhaps this event alone did not lead to its abandonment; but Hamwic's trading partners were also being raided, and trade must have suffered

A view of the St. Mary's area of Southampton with St. Mary's church in the foreground and the river Itchen in the background.

considerably as a result. Yet there is some evidence that other towns like Rouen (raided in 841) and Quentovic ('devastated', according to one chronicler, in 842) survived as towns; and there is no evidence to suggest Hamwic was more vulnerable than them.

Broad changes in the economic system of Wessex were probably acting against the continuation of towns like Hamwic. Other centres, in particular London, may have been attracting the trade that had previously gone to Hamwic. In part, Hamwic's decline and disappearance may be explained by the growing importance of Winchester during the 9th century. That town became the seat of the king and his court, and seems to have taken over Hamwic's role as an administrative centre. If Hamwic was like any Medieval town, it could maintain its numbers only through new people moving into the town. With Winchester growing in importance, people may have chosen not to settle in Hamwic. In that case, the town would eventually have withered away.

What became of the population? We know that the town was not to become one of the small defended towns, known as

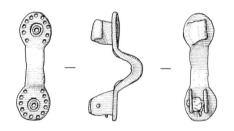

burhs, established throughout Wessex in the later 9th century. Nevertheless, there was a burh in the area. The Roman fort of Clausentum, on the east bank of the River Itchen, may have been reused as a burghal fort. But, unlike Hamwic, it did not have the characteristics of a town. Some of the population may have removed themselves to the new centre, some seem to have stayed at Hamwic, others probably settled in Winchester. Whatever happened exactly, the area of the Medieval walled town was not immediately occupied. Not until the last half of the 10th century was some attempt made to establish a settlement there, and the settlement had few characteristics of a town at first.

When excavations began in Southampton over 40 years ago, the main aims were to examine and describe the Saxon and Medieval towns and uncover any links that may have existed between them. Excavation has been successful in the first aim but to a large extent the relationships between the end of the Hamwic and the growth of the Medieval town is still unclear. We believe that there was an interval of a century between the end of Hamwic as a town and the establishment of some sort of settlement along the higher and more easily defensible land at the mouth of the River Test. What happened during those 100 years is still to be discovered.

Late Saxon brooches from Southampton.

CONCLUSION

The Saxon town of Hamwic, once lost in all but a few fleeting references, has been rediscovered after many years of archaeological excavations. The physical appearance of the town, life in the home, and the industrious activities of the community are well represented by the physical remains and artefacts left in the ground.

But there are elements of life in the town which remain elusive and others still very contentious. The minds and morality of the people, their political and familial relationships, though glimpsed at from documentary and archaeological sources, remain largely unknown. And some elements of the picture presented here are only the most likely interpretation of the material available. Other interpretations are possible and in time our picture of Hamwic may change. But for the main part we can be content with a lucid picture of the Saxon town of Hamwic, whose only monument to its existence is the church of St Mary protecting the dead of Hamwic who lie beside it.

BIBLIOGRAPHY

Andrews, P, forthcoming
Excavations at Hamwic, vol II
Bourdillon, J (ed), forthcoming
The Environment and Economy of Southampton
Fell, C, 1985 *Women in Anglo-Saxon England*
Hodges, R, 1981 *The Hamwic Pottery*, CBA research report 37
——, 1982
Dark Age Economics
Hunter, J, and Heyworth, M, forthcoming
Southampton Finds, vol II: the glass
Metcalf, DM, and Timby, J, in press
Southampton Finds, vol I: the coins and pottery of Hamwic
Morton, A, forthcoming
Excavations at Hamwic, vol I
Wilson, D, 1981 *The Anglo Saxons*

St. Mary's Church.

ACKNOWLEDGEMENTS

This booklet was produced by Southampton City Museums Archaeology Section. Particular thanks are due to Phil Andrews and Alan Morton, whose research into the Middle Saxon town of Hamwic was the main source for the information contained in this booklet. Thanks are also due to the following specialist researchers who have spent many years studying the material from Hamwic and whose findings have enriched our interpretations and image of the Saxon town:

Mary Alexander, Justine Bayley, Brian Biddle, Jennifer Bourdillon, Sarah Colley, Pete Cottrell, Jenny Coy, Richard Darrah, Anne Fahy, Vanessa Fell, Frank Green, Mike Heyworth, David Hinton, John Hunter, Michael Metcalf, Gerry Mcdonnel, David Peacock, Frances Pritchard, Ian Riddler, Jane Timby, David Williams, and Jessica Winder.

Finally, for their valuable comments and support, I should like to thank Mark Brisbane, Senior Keeper of Archaeology, Sian Jones, Museum Education Officer, and John Oxley, Assistant Archaeological Officer.